hugs for dad

hugs for dad

a loving look at fatherhood

www.youaretheauthor.com

ABC
Books

Published in Australia by ABC Books for the
AUSTRALIAN BROADCASTING CORPORATION
GPO Box 9994 Sydney NSW 2001

First published August 2008

Conceived and created by
Axis Publishing Limited
8c Accommodation Road
London NW11 8ED
www.axispublishing.co.uk

Creative Director: Siân Keogh
Editorial Director: Anne Yelland
Designer: Simon de Lotz
Production Manager: Jo Ryan

ISBN 978 0 7333 2277 8

Printed and bound in China
5 4 3 2 1

about this book

He's a rock to lean on, a shoulder to cry on, and a friend to rely on. Your dad is as important as your mum, but probably gets told so less often and less vociferously. This book is the ideal gift for dads. Its collection of witty and wise sayings on dads and fatherhood, compiled from the thoughts of people of all ages from around the world, demonstrates the important place fathers hold in the lives of their sons and daughters. Complemented by amusing animal photographs, it is the ideal way to say "Thanks" and "I love you."

about the author

Why have one author when you can have the world? This book has been compiled using the incredible resource that is the world wide web. From the many hundreds of contributions that were sent to the website *www.youaretheauthor.com* we have selected the ones that best sum up what being a father is all about.

Please continue to send your special views, feelings and advice about life – you never know you too might see your words of wisdom in print one day.

The older I get, the smarter my father gets.

You didn't tell me
how to live…

…you showed me.

anon@youaretheauthor.com

Nobody hears what
a father says to his
kids, but it will be
heard by posterity.

Scratch any father and you'll find someone chock full of qualms and romantic terrors.

Dads accept us as
we are yet help us to
be what we should be.

anon@youaretheauthor.com

The trouble with fathers is that by the time they are experienced, they are unemployed.

A rich man is one whose children run into his arms when his hands are empty.

To recapture your youth,
cut off his allowance.

Fathers are the powers that be.

anon@youaretheauthor.com

You can call your
dad at 4 a.m. and
he won't mind.

anon@youaretheauthor.com

A wise father knows
his own child.

anon@youaretheauthor.com

Dads want to stop you making mistakes, but still let you find your own way.

A father is a banker
provided by nature.

anon@youaretheauthor.com

The father who does not teach his son his duties is equally guilty with the son who neglects them.

There's a special place in heaven for a dad who takes his daughter shopping.

anon@youaretheauthor.com

Be kind to your father:
when you were young,
he loved you so much.

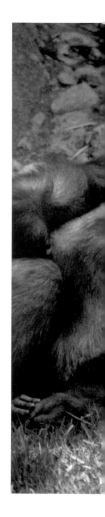

anon@youaretheauthor.com

We don't need to speak to understand each other perfectly.

Dad laughs at your jokes when they're not so good, and sympathises with your problems when they're not so bad.

anon@youaretheauthor.com

It is not flesh and blood
but the heart which makes
us fathers and sons.

A father provides
everything.

Whatever else you do in life, being a dad makes you most proud.

Dad's arms are always open.

A father is not so much a father as a walking encyclopedia.

A man never stands
as tall as when he
kneels to help a child.

To his daughter, a father
is a pat of butter in a hot pan.

My dad is a blessing
from heaven.

Father's Day is like Mother's Day, only you don't spend as much.

anon@youaretheauthor.com

Father is another
word for love.

anon@youaretheauthor.com

With your dad,
you can sit on a porch,
never saying a word,
and walk away feeling
like that was the best
conversation you've had.

anon@youaretheauthor.com

A father carries pictures
where his money used to be.

anon@youaretheauthor.com

When you teach your son,
you teach your son's son.

anon@youaretheauthor.com

Fathers are the mountains
we call home.

It doesn't matter
what your father is…

…what matters is what
you remember him to be.

What a dad teaches
at odd moments is more
important than what he
teaches when he's
trying to teach.

A father expects
his children to be as good
as he meant to be.

A father knows when he
is getting old, because he starts
to look like his father.

All kids need their
father's protection.

anon@youaretheauthor.com

You never grow out of needing your dad.

The poorest man can leave his children the richest inheritance.

You have to do your own growing, no matter how tall your father is.

anon@youaretheauthor.com

Dad, the best thing
you taught me was
that laughter is the
best medicine.

By the time a man realises that maybe his father was right, he usually has a son who thinks he's wrong.

If you want to keep
your kids, let them go.

There are three stages of a man's life: he believes in Santa Claus, he doesn't believe in Santa Claus, he is Santa Claus.

Being a dad is a privilege.

Dads hand their kids
the script for life.

anon@youaretheauthor.com

If your children look up to you, you've made a success of life's biggest job.

The worst misfortune
that can happen to an
ordinary man is to have
an extraordinary father.

No man can equal your father:
so great, so good, so faultless.

The most important thing
a father teaches his children is
how to get along without him.

anon@youaretheauthor.com

Fathers represent another way of looking at life – the possibility of an alternative dialogue.

anon@youaretheauthor.com

The sooner you treat
your son like a man,
the sooner he will be one.

My dad gave me the
greatest gift…

…he believed in me.

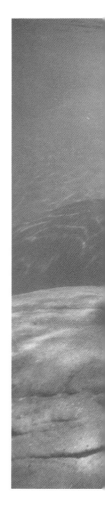

anon@youaretheauthor.com

Whatever a dad does, he's right at least 50 percent of the time.

anon@youaretheauthor.com

A father's worth more
than a hundred teachers.

The most important thing
a father can do for his children
is to love their mother.

It's only when you move away that you can measure your father's greatness and fully appreciate it.

A man's children and his garden both reflect the amount of weeding done during the growing season.

It's impossible to please the whole world and your dad.

Dad's love makes you
dance through the days.

anon@youaretheauthor.com